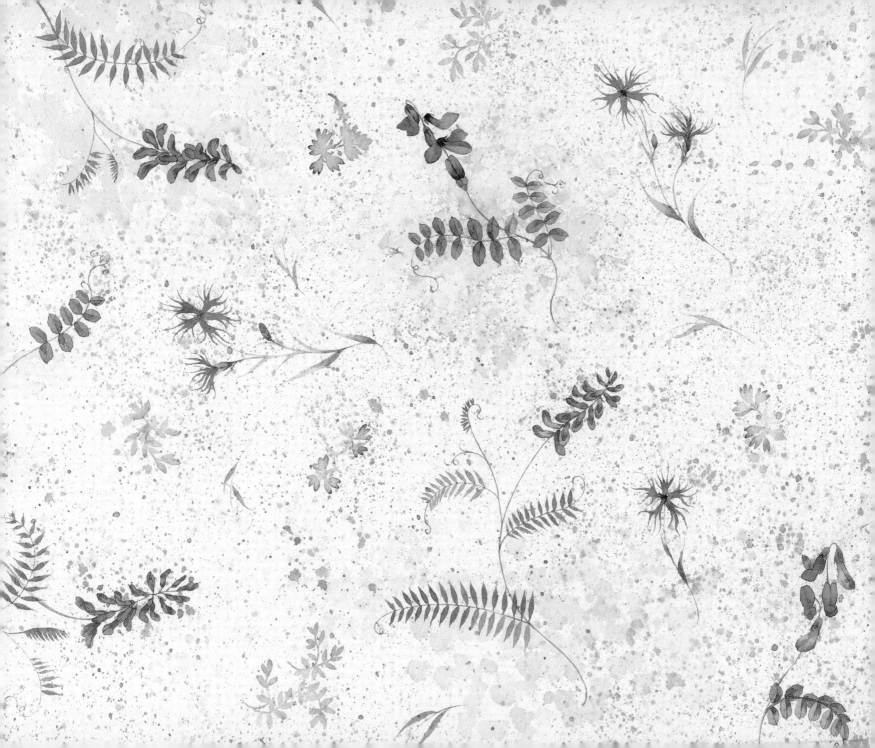

To Margaret

The author would like to thank the Staffordshire Wildlife Rescue
and Rehabilitation Centre for resource material,
Rosemary Lanning and Bob Eames for their creative input and
Tony, Patrick and James for accompanying her 'Down the Lane'.

First published 2001 by Happy Cat Books, Bradfield, Essex CO11 2UT

A CIP catalogue record for this book is available from the British Library

ISBN 1 903285 17 8 Paperback
ISBN 1 903285 18 6 Hardback

Printed in Hong Kong by Wing King Tong Co. Ltd.

Down the Lane

Sights and Sounds through the Seasons

Valerie Greeley

Happy Cat Books

*D*own the lane in January

I heard a fox's cry

As the first stars of the evening

Lit the twilight sky.

I saw a clump of snowdrops

In a bed of filigree

As the piercing, icy wind

Shook the ancient tree.

Down the lane in February
I heard the blackbird's mellow tone
While the hedgehog and the dormouse
Slept as cold as stone.

I saw shining stars of Celandine
Reflect the pale sunlight
And a yellow brimstone butterfly
Spread his wings for flight.

Down the lane in March
I heard the rustle of a mole
Digging with four shovel feet,
Coat as black as coal.

I saw a March hare racing,
Trying to catch the breeze
And a clutch of speckled eggs
Cradled in ivy leaves.

*D*own the lane in April

I heard the cuckoo sing

In blossom-laden branches,

Herald of the spring.

I saw a hedgehog shuffling

Through a forest of flowers

Made fragrant by glistening raindrops,

Fresh from April showers.

*D*own the lane in May

I heard a fledgling call

And underneath the chestnut tree

Watched the blossom fall.

I saw a young grey rabbit

Beneath the hawthorn's shade

For a moment resting there

Sheltered in the glade.

Down the lane in June

I heard the murmuring of bees,

Seeking nectar from the roses

Growing through the trees.

I saw the sun sink slowly

Towards the end of day

Whilst a family of badgers

Enjoyed their silent play.

Down the lane in July

I heard the cooing of a dove

As the storm clouds gathered

In the sky above.

I saw a dragonfly darting

Over harebells slender and blue

And a young toad, exploring worlds

Dangerous and new.

*D*own the lane in August

I heard a wasp pass by,

Charting a secret pathway

Through the summer sky.

I saw a long-tailed field mouse

Sitting in a nest, now bare,

As the swifts began to gather

In the sultry air.

Down the lane in September
I heard the skylark sing.
Rising over the morning mist
It soared on beating wing.

I saw a field of mushrooms
Growing through an ivy floor
And a squirrel, harvesting
From the hedgerow's store.

*D*own the lane in October

I heard the crackle of dry leaves,

Lying crisp upon the ground,

Stirred up by the breeze.

I saw the hedgerow changing

Its colour from green to gold

As the nights drew ever longer

And the days grew cold.

Down the lane in November
I heard the cold wind groan
And far away a shooting star
Crossed the sky alone.

I saw the ancient hawthorn
Outlined in shimmering light,
Its branches white and ghostly
In the frosty night.

*D*own the lane in December

I heard singing loud and clear –

A robin's lonely tribute

To the dying year.

I saw the snowflakes whirling

As if to make a ring

Around a single snowdrop,

Omen of the spring.

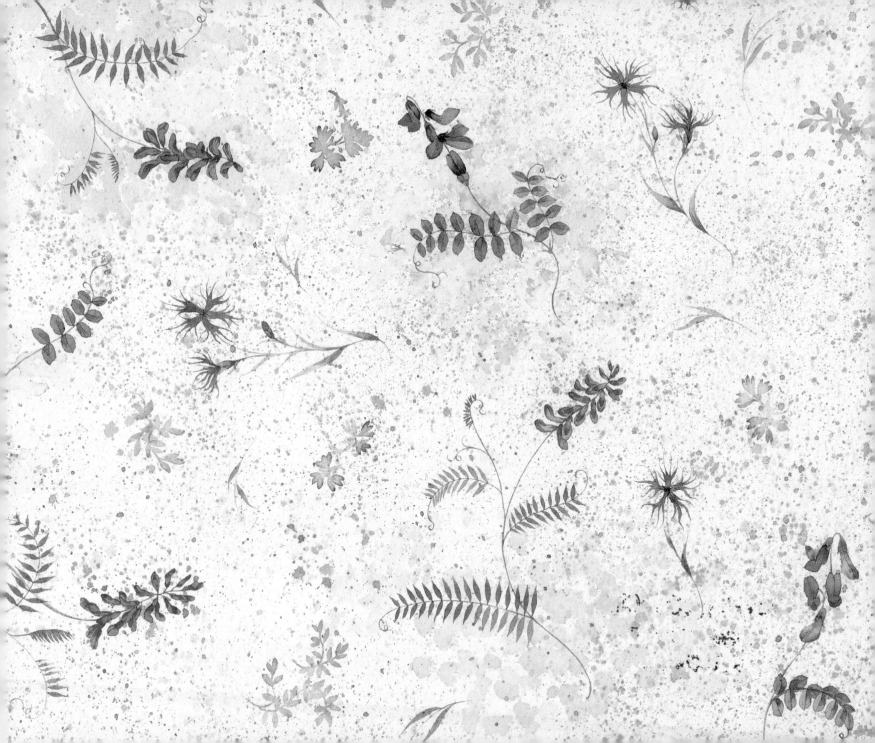